"OH, MARY!"
BY
COLE ESCOLA

PRODUCTION CREDITS

OH, MARY! premiered at the Lucille Lortel Theatre in New York City in January 2024. It was directed by Sam Pinkleton, the set design was by dots, the costume design was by Holly Pierson, the lighting design was by Cha See, the sound design was by Daniel Kluger and Drew Levy, the wig design was by Leah J. Loukas, the original music was by Daniel Kluger, the arrangements were by David Dabbon, and the production stage manager was Bryan Bauer. The cast was as follows:

MARY TODD LINCOLN	Cole Escola
MARY'S HUSBAND	Conrad Ricamora
MARY'S CHAPERONE	Bianca Leigh
MARY'S HUSBAND'S ASSISTANT	Tony Macht
MARY'S TEACHER	James Scully
UNDERSTUDIES	Peter Smith, Hannah Solow

OH, MARY! transferred to Broadway's Lyceum Theatre in June 2024 with the same cast and creative team. It was produced by Kevin McCollum & Lucas McMahon and Mike Lavoie & Carlee Briglia, and coproduced by Bob Boyett, The Council, Jean Doumanian Productions, Nicole Eisenberg, Jay Marcus & George Strus, Irony Point, Richard Batchelder / Bradley Reynolds, Tyler Mount / Tommy Doyle, Nelson & Tao, Palomares & Rosenberg, and ShowTown Productions.

COVER ART CREDITS

TITLE DESIGN	Teddy Blanks
PHOTO	Daniel Rampulla
GOWN	Astor Yang
HAIR	Jameson Eaton
MAKEUP	Angelo Balassone

CHARACTERS

MARY TODD LINCOLN

MARY'S HUSBAND (ABRAHAM)

MARY'S CHAPERONE (LOUISE, also plays BILL)

MARY'S HUSBAND'S ASSISTANT (SIMON, also plays KYLE)

MARY'S TEACHER (JOHN)

NOTES

1. Protect all of the surprises of the show.

2. Don't let the audience get ahead of the story.

3. The stakes are high and everyone means what they say.

OH, MARY!

Scene 1

Abraham Lincoln's office. There is a desk, a bookshelf, a couch, a window, and a portrait of George Washington. Abraham enters with a military aid, Simon.

ABRAHAM. Give me the latest from General Cooper!

SIMON. No updates from General Cooper, Mister President.

ABRAHAM. What about Thomas and his men?

SIMON. No updates from General Thomas eith—

ABRAHAM. God, we're screwed! We might as well surrender and kill ourselves now!

SIMON. Have faith, sir! Cooper and Thomas are two of the best Generals we've got. They've led us to multiple victories in the South.

ABRAHAM. Damn it, this isn't the South we're dealing with, it's my wife!

SIMON. I understand, sir.

ABRAHAM. No you don't. No one is safe while my wife has access to booze. The last time this happened she scaled a clock tower, derailed a freight train, and took a piss all over the Senate floor.

Abraham and Simon begin searching for something.

She was last spotted sneaking a bottle of whiskey into this house. She hid it somewhere and until we find it we—

Abraham finds the bottle behind a couch cushion.

Victory.

SIMON. Congratulations, sir! Shall I call off our men?

ABRAHAM. Yes!

Abraham puts the bottle in the drawer of his desk.

SIMON. Good! In the meantime, sir, we should meet with General Burnside to discuss the latest from the front lines.

ABRAHAM. Let's go. After dealing with my foul and hateful wife all morning a little war might be a breath of fresh air.

SIMON. I'm sure she means well, sir.

> *They exit. Mary Todd Lincoln bursts into the office, snarling, growling. She rushes to the couch cushion and lifts it to discover the bottle she hid is gone.*

MARY. No!

> *She checks behind other cushions.*

No no no no no no! *(To Abraham's desk.)* Oh you bastard! You pig! *(To the portrait of George Washington.)* Oh, Mother, why did I marry him?!

> *Mary begins thrashing the papers on Abraham's desk.*

Bastard! Pig! Bastard! Pig!

> *She discovers a gun in his desk, stares at it a moment, then puts it back, disapprovingly, then gives a final thrash.*

Bastard!

> *She starts to leave the office pouting/crying/whimpering. Through her sniffles she smells something. Huh… She sniffs again and continues sniffing, like a truffle pig, on a trail to the desk drawer where Abraham has put the bottle of whiskey. AHA! It's in there! Assuming the drawer is locked, she grabs a letter opener from the desk and tries to stab the drawer open. No dice. She grabs a big book from the shelf and uses it like a hammer on the letter opener to try and pry the drawer open. No dice again. She drops the book and the letter opener and grabs a fire poker. She swings it like a baseball bat and bashes the desk drawer three times to no avail. She drops to her knees and hollers in defeat. She gets up from the ground, bracing herself on the drawer handle. This causes the drawer to open. It was never locked at all. Victory! She grabs the bottle and is about to open it when she hears:*

ABRAHAM. *(Offstage.)* God damn them!

Uh-oh. She peeks out the door. He's coming. She looks around the room, not knowing what to do.

MARY. *(To George.)* Oh, Mother!

She grabs the big book and lays down on the couch, resting the book on top of the bottle on top of her, and pretends to be asleep.

Abraham enters on a tear, reading some bad news.

ABRAHAM. God damn their whole goddamned army! And God damn Robert E. Lee! *(To God.)* Oh Dear Heavenly Father, please, I beg you to show me what I can do to— *(Seeing Mary.)* Oh Jesus Christ. *(To God.)* Sorry. *(Seeing her.)* Mary.

Mary "snores." He's not buying this scene.

Mary.

Mary "stirs in her sleep." Abraham approaches her hatefully.

Mary!

Mary "wakes up."

MARY. AHH! Oh my God! Abraham! I must have fallen asleep while I was reading my book.

ABRAHAM. Really? Good book?

MARY. Oh yes.

Abraham reaches for the book, Mary pulls it away.

No! You wouldn't like it. It's very sad. You hate sad stories.

ABRAHAM. Not at all, I love sad stories.

Right as Mary has stealthily moved the bottle behind her, Abraham grabs the book.

(Reading.) Webster's Dictionary.

MARY. Poor Webster. Murdered on his birthday.

ABRAHAM. *(Seeing his desk.)* God damn it! What the hell / happened to my desk?!

MARY. / What happened to your desk?

ABRAHAM. I thought drunks were supposed to be good liars.

MARY. What?

ABRAHAM. You're a terrible actress, Mary.

Abraham tries to put his office back together.

MARY. How dare you! I'm offended! I am leaving!

Mary grabs the bottle with a pillow to hide it.

ABRAHAM. Stop! What are you holding?

MARY. Simply a pillow.

ABRAHAM. Why are you taking a pillow with you?

MARY. I want to show it to my friends.

ABRAHAM. You don't have friends.

MARY. I know. I'm hoping to make some. By going into town and showing everyone my amazing pillow.

Abraham grabs the pillow.

Ow! Stop! The baby! The baby?

Abraham rips the pillow out of Mary's hands, revealing the bottle. Abraham grabs the bottle and they tug-of-war. With a strong pull, Abraham gains control of the bottle.

ABRAHAM. God damn it, Mary! Where's Louise?

MARY. She went home.

ABRAHAM. Mary! What did you do to Louise?

MARY. Nothing! Why, what did she say? She's a liar!

ABRAHAM. Mary.

MARY. Why would I throw an entire woman down the stairs? Because it's hilarious? That doesn't make any sense. It was an accident! It could've happened to anybody I wanted to get rid of. Besides, I don't need a babysitter.

ABRAHAM. Louise is a companion. She likes you.

MARY. No she doesn't. Not after I threw her down the stairs.

ABRAHAM. Get the hell out of my sight, I have too much to do.

MARY. I swear to God I'm going to leave this place.

ABRAHAM. Oh good. Where are you going?

MARY. West.

ABRAHAM. California?

MARY. The liquor store.

ABRAHAM. Oh stop it. You can make me out to be the villain all you want but I'm thinking of your health.

MARY. You're thinking of your reputation. And what good is being healthy when you spend your life in a cage? It's like having gorgeous shoes and no feet.

ABRAHAM. You need to be active. Get a hobby, something you can throw yourself into.

MARY. I had that and you took it away from me.

ABRAHAM. Aside from whiskey.

MARY. I don't mean whiskey.

ABRAHAM. Then what?

MARY. You know what. The only thing I care about in this whole world!

ABRAHAM. The children?

   Abraham and Mary laugh.

MARY. Please, Abraham. You know what matters to me. Let me go back.

ABRAHAM. Oh Jesus Christ, not this again! You wanted out when you met me, remember!

MARY. Well now I've met you enough and I want back in!

ABRAHAM. No! I forbid it. You are not going back to that.

MARY. It has a name.

ABRAHAM. It doesn't deserve one.

MARY. Say it!

ABRAHAM. No.

MARY. The thing I love more than anything on earth is—

ABRAHAM. Don't say it!

MARY. Cabaret!

ABRAHAM. That's it! Out!

MARY. Please! Let me go back to it, Abe!

ABRAHAM. No! It's inappropriate! We're at war!

MARY. With who?

ABRAHAM. The South!

MARY. Of what?

ABRAHAM. Forget it! Do something else. Horseback riding.

MARY. No! I hate those horses. They laugh at me.

ABRAHAM. We've been over this, Mary, they're neighing. Horses neigh.

MARY. You always take their side!

ABRAHAM. Enough! I'll have Louise come by tomorrow to give you some painting lessons.

MARY. Painting lessons? Jesus Christ!

ABRAHAM. You're being unreasonable.

MARY. And you're being unSEASONABLE. Unseasonably COLD. You snowman! You ice bastard!

ABRAHAM. Get out!

Mary grabs her head.

MARY. Ow!

ABRAHAM. What?

Mary puts her hands on her head like the pressure is unbearable.

MARY. I can't—ow! Ow! My femur! My femur!

ABRAHAM. Your femur is in your leg, Mary.

MARY. It's pushing up into my head! I'm bleeding! I'm bleeding!

ABRAHAM. You're not bleeding.

MARY. Oh God! I'm hallucinating blood! That's a sign of dehydration! Quick, give me a drink of whatever is near!

ABRAHAM. 1...2...

MARY. No! I'm good girl. I'm good girl. I wish we really were at war.

Blackout.

Scene 2

Abraham is perched on his desk, midstory to Simon.

ABRAHAM. And then I said, how about we call it "The Gettysburg Address."

SIMON. Wow. That's a great story, sir.

ABRAHAM. Thank you, Simon. Take a letter to General Thomas immediately.

SIMON. Another letter, sir?

ABRAHAM. What do you mean?

SIMON. You just wrote him a letter.

ABRAHAM. I did? Oh, yes. Show it to me.

SIMON. Yes, sir.

> *Simon riffles through papers in his hands and drops some. He bends to pick them up and Abraham stares at his behind.*

ABRAHAM. Fuck…

> *Mary enters. Simon, still bent over, notices her. Abraham, still staring at Simon, does not.*

SIMON. Sir. Your wife.

ABRAHAM. I wasn't looking at you, I was looking at the floor!

SIMON. What?

ABRAHAM. What?

SIMON. *(Pointing.)* Your wife.

ABRAHAM. Oh. Mary.

MARY. Sorry to disturb. I just need a book.

ABRAHAM. What book?

MARY. Just something to weigh the easel down so it doesn't blow over in the wind.

ABRAHAM. How about *Webster's Dictionary*.

MARY. Perfect. Well have a wonderful afternoon, gentlemen.

> *Mary takes the book and exits.*

SIMON. Afternoon, ma'am. *(To Abraham.)* Your wife paints?

ABRAHAM. She's taking lessons. Did she seem unusually chipper to you?

SIMON. She seemed happy, I guess.

ABRAHAM. What the hell is she up to? Never mind. Take a letter to General Thomas immediately.

SIMON. Sir, you already—

ABRAHAM. Oh! Right! Damn it. I'm falling apart. I can't eat, I can't sleep. This goddamn war has me so tense I can't even think clearly. And that fucking witch!

SIMON. Relax, sir. We need you in peak form.

ABRAHAM. You're right, Simon. Maybe I need to take a break. Let off some steam.

SIMON. I think that's a very good idea, sir.

ABRAHAM. Do you?

SIMON. Yes.

ABRAHAM. You want to see me let off some steam?

SIMON. That would make me very happy, sir.

ABRAHAM. Would it? Would it put a big smile on your face to see me release everything I've got pent up?

SIMON. Of course. I want you to take it easy, sir.

ABRAHAM. Oh I'll take it easy. And you'll take it hard.

SIMON. I don't follow you, sir.

ABRAHAM. Oh you're good. "I don't follow you, sir." I bet you don't. Okay. You wanna play the coy, naive little schoolgirl? Fine, let's play. You're at school and you need glasses but your family can't afford them, lucky for you I'm an optometrist without a conscience.

> *Louise, a very prim and proper woman, barges in holding a bucket.*

LOUISE. Code red, coming through.

> *A very intoxicated Mary stumbles in behind her, cackling and holding a small jar. Abraham and Simon help get her to the couch.*

ABRAHAM. God damn it.

SIMON. What happened?!

ABRAHAM. Whiskey? Vodka?

LOUISE. Paint thinner.

SIMON. I'll fetch a doctor at once!

LOUISE and ABRAHAM. No.

> *Abraham pries the jar out of Mary's hand.*

ABRAHAM. It looks like she didn't drink much.

LOUISE. That's water. This was the paint thinner.

SIMON. Good God! She's going to die!

> *Abraham and Louise go to Abraham's desk and mix a concoction consisting of a bottle of this and a few shakes of that. They have this process down* pat.

LOUISE. Not on my watch.

ABRAHAM. If drinking a bucket of paint thinner could kill my wife she would've died a long time ago.

LOUISE. You poor, poor man. I don't know how you do it.

ABRAHAM. I should have married you, Louise.

LOUISE. Oh, Mister President.

ABRAHAM. Good, kind, noble.

LOUISE. Oh, Mister President.

MARY. Oh Jesus Christ!

SIMON. Sir, please! Let me fetch a doctor! This isn't normal!

ABRAHAM. Shut the fuck up! She just needs to drink this.

> *Abraham crosses to her with the drink. She's out cold.*

Mary… Mary…

SIMON. She's not responsive!

> *Abraham and Louise share a look. Louise knocks on Abraham's desk.*

LOUISE and ABRAHAM. Places, Miss Todd.

> *Mary shoots awake long enough to take a drink. She vomits in the bucket.*

SIMON and LOUISE. Oh!

> *Mary passes back out. Then comes to, vomits again.*

Oh!

> *Mary passes back out. Then comes to, almost vomits again, but sneezes instead.*

Aww.

ABRAHAM. Go, we'll be all right.

LOUISE. I'll come by tomorrow with an activity that doesn't include any toxic solvents.

ABRAHAM. Thank you, Louise. Goodbye.

SIMON. Shall I leave too, sir?

ABRAHAM. Uh. Yes.

> *Simon and Louise exit.*

Damn it! *(Praying.)* Dear God, forgive me for what I almost did with Simon. I am under so much pressure, Lord. Please oh please, win me this war, Lord, and keep my wife from ruining my name. Just give me those two things and I swear to you right here and now…I swear that I will never do anything homosexual ever again. Please, please, please, please, please!

> *Mary comes to, grabs the bucket, then begins drinking from it. Abraham hears her glug-glug-glug and turns around.*

Mary!

> *Mary sticks out her tongue with a smile, refreshed.*

MARY. Aaaah.

> *Blackout.*

Scene 3

> *Louise is seated at a needlepoint frame with a canvas on it, demonstrating for Mary.*

LOUISE. And bring the needle up through the spot where you would like your knot to be. Now when we actually begin this piece,

I suggest we start here, where the grass will be, but for the sake of learning, we'll just start right here so you can get the idea. How does that sound?

MARY. Amazing.

LOUISE. Now, take the needle and point it away from your work. Then you're going to wrap your thread around the needle once, then twice, and then turn—

MARY. *(To scare Louise.)* BAH!

LOUISE. AAAH! Oh my goodness! Why on earth did you do that?!

MARY. Louise, even if I knew, I wouldn't tell you.

LOUISE. My heart! It's flapping like a hummingbird. You really scared me!

MARY. Do it to me, Louise. Scare me. I want to feel my heart flapping. I want to feel something, anything! I'm so bored. Nothing ever happens around here.

LOUISE. Nothing ever happens? Our country is at war! Thousands are being ravaged by typhoid. Your own son perished just last year.

MARY. It's no use trying to make me laugh, Louise. I feel so—so—

LOUISE. So what?

MARY. Exactly. I feel so "So what!" Louise, what would you do if you had no responsibilities? If you had everything you needed and didn't have to answer to anything or anyone. What would you do?

LOUISE. Exactly what I'm doing now.

MARY. Oh come on. You don't even have a little secret wish? Some wild dream you don't tell anyone? *(Off Louise's silence.)* Louise? Why, Louise! You do!

LOUISE. No.

MARY. Yes! Just now, I saw a smile behind those eyes.

LOUISE. A smile happens with the mouth, not the eyes.

MARY. Oh shut up, dumbass, you know what I meant! Tell me. Tell me what it is you dream of doing.

LOUISE. I can't.

MARY. You can and you will or I'll stab these needles in your eyes and you know I'll do it!

LOUISE. But it's so shameful. If anyone ever found out, I would simply die!

MARY. No one will find out! Please, Louise. I'm so miserable. It would help me so much to hear your secret and feel like I'm not alone.

LOUISE. Oh. All right. But you must promise not to tell anyone!

MARY. Cross my heart and hope to die!

LOUISE. And you mustn't laugh!

MARY. Me? Laugh? Ha!

LOUISE. Okay. I—I can't!

MARY. Louise!

LOUISE. Okay! Okay. If I had no ties and no responsibilities, the thing I would want most is…ice cream.

MARY. Ice cream?

LOUISE. Yes.

MARY. That's your big secret wild dream? Eating ice cream?

LOUISE. No. Not eating it…

MARY. Yeah, you are going to have to explain further.

LOUISE. Please understand that I came upon this discovery purely by accident. But last summer while I was enjoying a nice big cone of vanilla ice cream, it was piled way too high and as I brought it to my mouth, a scoop of it fell off into my lap and—oh my God! The sensation! First sharp. Then numb. Then tingles. Tingles everywhere.

MARY. Tingles from ice cream on your thigh?

LOUISE. No, not my thigh. Higher.

MARY. Your stomach?

LOUISE. Lower.

MARY. Lower than your stomach, higher than your thigh… *(Gasps!)* You mean…

LOUISE. Yes. Remember, not a soul.

> *Abraham enters.*

ABRAHAM. We won the war!

MARY. Louise wants to rub ice cream on her pussy!

LOUISE. Mary! Mister President! What she says—it isn't true! I never—!

ABRAHAM. Did you hear what I—

MARY. I asked her what she longed for more than anything in the world and she told me some stupid story about dropping ice cream on her crotch and loving it!

LOUISE. No! You—you misunderstood! Mister President! I'm—

ABRAHAM. Louise, you don't have to explain. I know better than anyone the extent of my wife's disgusting imagination.

MARY. Does it have to be vanilla, Louise, have you tried it with strawberry? Or would the seeds get stuck in your—

LOUISE. Please excuse me. I have matters at home to attend to. That's wonderful news about the war, Mister President. I'm so happy to hear it. Good day.

     Louise exits.

ABRAHAM. Forgive my wife, Louise! Come back soon!

MARY. Hey she's a hoot, huh?

ABRAHAM. Mary.

MARY. Abraham! The war is over! Now I can do cabaret!

ABRAHAM. No. But I have given it some thought and I've decided—

MARY. But you said cabaret was inappropriate because we're at war but the—

ABRAHAM. Will you let me finish?!

MARY. Will you let me start?! Abraham, tell me what has changed with you? You used to love cabaret. You always said you loved my madcap medleys!

ABRAHAM. No, I said I heard your madcap medleys.

MARY. You were there every night! Singing along!

ABRAHAM. I was young and confused! Now let it go!

MARY. Why are you so ashamed? Cabaret brought us together. We fell in love at the cabaret!

ABRAHAM. You better not repeat that to anyone! We fell in love at a dance in Illinois. That's the story!

MARY. What's wrong with you loving cabaret?!

ABRAHAM. I don't love cabaret! Stop saying that! It makes me look like a—like a—

MARY. Like a what? Like a fan of elegant stories told through song? That's a wonderful thing to be! We should tell the whole country, "Abraham Lincoln loves cabaret!"

ABRAHAM. Will you shut up about cabaret for one second and listen to me?! I'm trying to ask you about the theatre!

MARY. What about the theatre?

ABRAHAM. Are you ready to listen?

MARY. Yes.

ABRAHAM. And you won't interrupt me?

MARY. No.

ABRAHAM. It isn't—

MARY. But why does—Sorry. Go ahead.

ABRAHAM. Cabaret is not—

MARY. You said that—Sorry. Nope. God, what is wrong with me? Sorry. I'm listening.

ABRAHAM. Cabaret is…

MARY. A world-class art form—

ABRAHAM. Disgusting. It's not respectable. The theatre, while it's not exactly respectable either, has a certain air of cultural importance to it.

MARY. Okay?

ABRAHAM. How would you feel about being an actress in the legitimate theatre?

MARY. Wait. You really mean it?

ABRAHAM. Yes.

MARY. Me? An actress? You'd really let me?!

ABRAHAM. I want you to be happy!

MARY. Wowie zowie! Where do we start?! You're producing a play for me to star in!

ABRAHAM. No.

MARY. Oh.

ABRAHAM. You see, I know how deeply you respect the arts, right?

MARY. Uh-huh.

ABRAHAM. And I assume if your goal is to be a great actress of the legitimate theatre, you will certainly want some sort of foundational training?

MARY. Uh-huh.

ABRAHAM. So I would like to pay for you to take acting lessons.

MARY. Uh-huh.

ABRAHAM. This will be an excellent opportunity to—

MARY. How stupid do you think I am?

ABRAHAM. Honestly?

MARY. In the first place, weirdo, I don't need acting lessons. There's no difference between theatre and cabaret. Theatre is just fewer feathers and flatter shoes! Second, I see right through this generous offer, Mister President. You have absolutely no intention of letting me on any stage, legitimate or otherwise. This is just another ploy to keep me from drinking and tucked away in the drawing room where no one can see me.

ABRAHAM. Contrary to what your paranoia tells you, I'm not some evil mastermind conspiring to keep you miserable.

MARY. When you keep me off the stage, you make the whole world miserable!

ABRAHAM. For God's sake, Mary! How would it look for the first lady of the United States to be flitting about a stage right now in the ruins of war!

MARY. How would it look?! Sensational!

ABRAHAM. Why are you so impossible?!

MARY. Why am I always the one to compromise? How soon after I take these lessons will you actually let me on a stage?

ABRAHAM. We'll cross that bridge when we come to it.

MARY. That means you'll burn that bridge before we get to it. God, I want a drink!

ABRAHAM. Will you open your stupid eyes? Do you know how hated I am right now? The nation is in ruins. The entire South hates me and half the North does too. That's three quarters of America against me. Hundreds of thousands of soldiers are dead. On both sides. So no, the president's wife will not be making her tone-deaf grand return to the stage anytime soon. But if she wants to drink, she should pour a glass tall enough to drown in. Because actually a dead wife would do wonders for the president's reputation in the South right now. Take the acting lessons, you fucking moron.

Mary gives up and exits, despondently. She reenters.

MARY. The South of what?

Blackout.

Scene 4

Mary fumes, mumbling to herself, playing out some rageful revenge fantasy. A knock at the door.

MARY. Come in!

John, handsome, charming, enters.

JOHN. Hello, ma'am.

Mary does a double take.

MARY. Fuck.

JOHN. You must be the first lady. It's a pleasure to meet you.

MARY. Why?

JOHN. Well, because it just is. I'm here to give acting lessons.

MARY. Congratulations.

JOHN. I'm sorry, I'm a little nervous. You see, I have experience acting but as far as teaching goes, it's fairly new for me. Completely new, in fact. This is my first time.

MARY. I'm not sure what you want me to say to that.

JOHN. Perhaps we should get started?

MARY. Knock yourself out, freak.

JOHN. Forgive me for being so forward, Madame First Lady, but do you not want me here?

MARY. Why should it bother you if I don't?

JOHN. Well, if it's something I said, or if there's anything I can do to help—

MARY. Yes, you can leave and never return.

JOHN. Of course. My apologies. Farewell, madame.

MARY. Wait! It's not your fault. I don't mean to be so—My husband set up these acting lessons. To keep me busy.

JOHN. Busy?

MARY. Yes. You see, I'm a rather well-known niche cabaret legend. Or I used to be, until my career was cut short by a love affair gone horribly right. Anyhow, I want to perform again but my husband resents it and finds me terribly annoying. So you're here to keep me out of his hair.

JOHN. I see. Well, I understand your resistance then, and I'm sorry.

MARY. No, I'm sorry for—for being a cunt.

JOHN. No, don't apologize. I thank you for your honesty. It's admirable. *(Then:)*
> "O! how much more doth beauty beauteous seem
> By that sweet ornament which truth doth give."

MARY. What?

JOHN. It's Shakespeare. Sonnet 54.

MARY. Ah yes!

JOHN. You like Sonnet 54?

MARY. Who wouldn't? Name a better sonnet that fits between 53 and 55.

JOHN. You're not too familiar with Shakespeare then.

MARY. Of course I am! "To be or not to be, that is a great question."

JOHN. I have a book of his sonnets with me. May I leave it here as a gift for you to keep?

MARY. Why?

JOHN. I think you might like it.

MARY. You don't know me.

JOHN. No, but—it will motivate me to read one of my other books for a change.

MARY. Well, thank you. That's incredibly kind, Mister—

JOHN. Oh! I'm sorry. I completely forgot to introduce myself. My name is Booth. John Wilkes Booth.

MARY. Thank you, Mister Booth.

> *John hands Mary the book. The book drops to the ground. They both bend to pick it up. John gets to it first. He looks up at Mary. Sparks. John gives her the book again and their hands touch.*

Please, don't drop my books like that.

JOHN. Pardon?

MARY. I just got this and now the corner is bent.

JOHN. Oh, my apologies.

MARY. It's okay, just be careful with my things. *(Reading from the book:)*

> "A man in hue, all hues in his controlling,
> Which steals men's eyes and women's souls amazeth.
> And for a woman wert thou first created,
> Till Nature as she wrought thee fell a-doting,"

(Then.) I guess that one's more of a "you had to be there" type of thing.

JOHN. I hope it brings you as much pleasure as it's brought me. Good day, ma'am.

> *John starts to leave.*

MARY. Mister Booth!

JOHN. Yes?

MARY. Just out of curiosity, what did you have in mind for our lesson today?

JOHN. Well, I thought we would start with scene work. Something befitting your type, of course.

MARY. What type is that?

JOHN. The romantic heroine, of course. Beatrice, Bianca, Juliet.

MARY. Oh come now, Mister Booth! I'm far too old for Juliet!

JOHN. Not for the sake of an acting lesson.

MARY. Oh. Thanks.

JOHN. Well, it was lovely meeting you. Good day!

> *John starts to leave again.*

MARY. Mister Booth!

JOHN. Yes?

MARY. I'm suddenly realizing, if you leave, I'll have nothing to do for my whole afternoon.

JOHN. Oh?

MARY. It's a terrible predicament, I'm afraid. You see, I don't do well with a lot of free time. I'm a drunk.

JOHN. Oh!

MARY. I mean—! Not a drunk! Just a, well I—it's a—I just don't do well with a lot of free time.

JOHN. I understand.

MARY. So perhaps, it would be in my best interest, if you stayed and we went ahead with your lesson as planned. I mean, after all, you're here.

JOHN. You're not just trying to be kind?

MARY. I wouldn't know how. Stay.

JOHN. It would be my pleasure.

MARY. You pushed me.

> *John sits on the other end of the couch from Mary.*

MARY. What made you want to teach acting?

JOHN. Well, I don't want to, sorry or—that is, I mean—

MARY. No, I understand. I don't even want to be alive.

JOHN. I am actually a professional actor. Or I would be, if I were better at it.

MARY. Oh nonsense. I'm sure you're marvelous. Booth. Wait a minute. Yes. I remember your name! I saw it on that big magnificent poster for *Hamlet* last year.

JOHN. That was my brother.

MARY. Oh. Then you're the other one! On the poster for *Julius Caesar* two seasons ago!

JOHN. That was my other brother.

MARY. Oh.

JOHN. But I was in that production.

MARY. Right!

JOHN. But my name wasn't on the poster.

MARY. Oh. Well just because your name's not on the poster doesn't mean you're not the star. Besides, I don't really remember those posters anyway. Remember, I'm a drunk.

JOHN. Thank you.

MARY. Oh no need to thank me, my drinking is completely compulsive. So where should we start?

JOHN. How about *The Tempest*?

> *John hands Mary another book, opened to a specific page.*

JOHN. Read from it. You be Miranda, I'll be Ferdinand. Start here.

MARY. Where?

JOHN. Here. Come. Begin.

MARY. *(Reading.)* "Alas now, pray you,
Work not so hard. I would the lightning had
Burnt up those logs that you are enjoined to pile!"

JOHN. Wow.

MARY. What?

JOHN. You read the role like a horny snake in a newspaper cartoon.

MARY. Thank you.

JOHN. But Miranda is a shy, innocent young girl.

MARY. Well why didn't you say so! I can do that!

JOHN. All right, continue.

MARY. "If you'll sit down,
    I'll bear your logs the while. Pray, give me that.
    I'll carry it to the pile."

JOHN. Stop. Not quite.

MARY. Well it's this part! Why is she so obsessed with logs?!

JOHN. It's not the logs she's after, she's in love with Ferdinand. Think of the subtext, this isn't a cabaret act.

MARY. How dare you look down your nose at cabaret. While you were "dost thou-ing" and "thine art-ing" for a cold dinner and a hard cot, I was taking my tenth and eleventh curtain calls, being showered with roses and rubies!

JOHN. I'm sorry I—

MARY. People traveled the world over for my short legs and long medleys. I had a hold over audiences the likes of which have not been seen since Christ disappeared from behind that stupid rock. My singing, thrilling; my personality, magnetic; my dancing, I made up for that with my singing and personality.

JOHN. I have no doubt you're talented. I can see the fire in you. But cabaret is different from theatre.

MARY. Oh what do you know about theatre! You're not even good enough to be on a poster! You're not even good enough to be acting right now! And I'm sure the acting jobs you did get probably only came because people thought you were one of your brothers. What's the saying? "Those who can't do, teach?" Maybe it ought to be "Those who can't do, don't!"

JOHN. All right. I'm so sorry I wasted your time and I certainly won't bother you again.

    John exits. Mary beats herself up.

MARY. Oh Mary, you boob!

    Blackout.

Scene 5

Abraham is seated at his desk, eyes shut, hands clasped, crying in prayer. Mary enters, unbeknownst to him.

ABRAHAM. Oh dear God. Dear God, please. Please, oh please, oh please, oh please!

MARY. Ahem.

ABRAHAM. Mary! What do you want?!

MARY. I love those acting lessons you gave me. In fact, I'd like more tomorrow.

ABRAHAM. Fine.

MARY. But I'm afraid I was rather unpleasant to Mister Booth so he might not want to come back.

ABRAHAM. I'm sure.

MARY. So please convey my apologies to him. If he refuses to come back, please tell him I'll be—

ABRAHAM. Mary, all I can do is ask! I'll see if he can come tomorrow. Now get out!

Mary exits. Abraham resumes his desperate prayer.

Oh dear God! Dear God, please. Please, please, please! Please, oh, please! Oh God, oh God, oh God, oh God, oh God, oh God, oh God! AAAHH!

Simon comes up from underneath Abraham's desk. (He wasn't praying after all, he was climaxing.)

SIMON. Is that what you meant, sir, when you said let off some steam?

ABRAHAM. Simon, that's exactly what I meant.

Blackout.

Scene 6

Mary stands, book in hand, rehearsing with Louise, who sits on the couch with a sack over her head.

MARY. "O gentle Romeo,
    If thou dost love, pronounce it faithfully.
    Or if thou think'st I am too quickly won,
    I'll frown and be perverse—"

    Louise laughs.

Louise!

LOUISE. What?

MARY. You're not supposed to laugh! It's a love scene.

LOUISE. Oh. Sorry. Can I please take this sack off of my head now? The smell is making me dizzy.

MARY. Fine. This is pointless anyway.

    Louise removes the sack from her head.

I'll never be an actress. No matter who or what I picture, I can't make myself feel what I'm saying. And if I can't feel it, how will anyone ever believe me?

LOUISE. I believed you!

MARY. You did?!

LOUISE. Yes, that's why I laughed.

MARY. Because you believed I was in love?

LOUISE. No, because I believed you were a horny snake in a newspaper cartoon!

MARY. Oh. Nothing I picture sets my heart ablaze the way Juliet's is supposed to be. If only I were you, Louise, then I know what I would picture.

LOUISE. What?

    Mary mimes licking an ice cream cone.

Stop it! I don't know why you care so much. You've never thrown yourself into a hobby this much before.

MARY. I'd like to show Mister Booth I can listen to him. I owe it to him. If he'll even come back. He's so good, Louise. The way he recites, his smile, the way he looks into my eyes, like he's known me all my life, longer.

LOUISE. Why don't you picture him for the love scene, then?

MARY. What?

LOUISE. If I didn't know any better I'd say you were in love with him. *(Off of Mary's shocked look.)* I'm only teasing.

MARY. Of course I'm not in love with him. That would be stupid. Let's try it again from the top. Sack back on your head, please.

LOUISE. What did you say this sack was used for?

MARY. Gardening stuff.

LOUISE. What stuff?

MARY. That stuff you put on flowers to help them grow.

LOUISE. Manure?!

MARY. Yes!

LOUISE. You made me wear a sack of animal poop?!

MARY. I'll laugh about that when you leave, Louise. Just put it back on.

LOUISE. No! I've had enough of your cruelty. You make fun of me, you throw me down the stairs, you set fire to my house on Christmas Eve!

MARY. I put it out!

LOUISE. On New Year's Day!

MARY. Louise, where are you going?

LOUISE. I hate to say this, Mary, but you asked for it! You are not nice!

Louise storms out. Abraham and Simon enter.

MARY. Louise! Don't just leave the sack here, Lou—Oh! Abraham! Did you get ahold of Mister Booth?

ABRAHAM. He has been invited back for lessons tomorrow at two.

MARY. Did he say he's coming?

ABRAHAM. I didn't see him directly, I only left word.

MARY. Well how will we know—

ABRAHAM. Mary, please! If he comes he comes, if he doesn't, you can go horseback riding with Louise!

MARY. No! I can't bear the smell of horse piss and moldy oats!

ABRAHAM. I'll have the stables cleaned.

MARY. I'm talking about Louise. Tomorrow, two o'clock. *(Rehearsing.)* "O Romeo, Romeo, wherefore art thou…" *(Forgetting the next line, reading it from her book.)* "Romeo?" Wait, that's it.

ABRAHAM. Mary, please leave.

MARY. I will. I just need you to give me those paints and brushes again.

ABRAHAM. Absolutely not.

MARY. I'm not going to drink paint thinner. Can't you see, I'm changed! Ugh, never mind, I'll find them myself.

>*Mary exits.*

ABRAHAM. Come in, Simon. Thank you for coming.

SIMON. Is something the matter, sir?

ABRAHAM. No. Yes. I wanted to apologize.

SIMON. Apologize?

ABRAHAM. For the other day when I—when the—when, you—

SIMON. When I used my mouth to make the sperm come out of your penis, sir?

ABRAHAM. Exactly. I want to apologize for that. That was, well, to put it rather bluntly, a big oopsie-daisy. I would very much prefer if we could forget that ever happened.

SIMON. Of course.

ABRAHAM. Thank you.

SIMON. As long as you don't forget the other part, sir.

ABRAHAM. Other part?

SIMON. What you said. About giving me a position in your cabinet.

ABRAHAM. Did I say that?

SIMON. Yes, sir.

ABRAHAM. I see. What else did I say?

SIMON. We discussed an increase in my salary as well, sir.

ABRAHAM. Right. Your position and your salary.

SIMON. And a pony.

ABRAHAM. A pony?

SIMON. For my sick daughter, sir.

ABRAHAM. Right. I will keep my word, Simon. No matter the state of mind I was in when I gave it to you.

SIMON. Thank you, sir. Is that all you wanted to see me about?

ABRAHAM. Yes. Yes, it is. Thank you.

Simon nods and exits. Abraham prays.

Dear God, I'm sorry. Thank you for winning the war for me and for keeping my wife busy. I swear to you, I swear, I swear, I swear I will hold up my end of the bargain too. No more gay. No more men… on their knees at my feet…looking up at me…with their wet, pink little mouths…like malnourished puppies desperate for my hot, sloppy milk—NO! I am done with that! And to prove I'm done, God, I am only going to do it one more time! Simon! Simon, come back!

Abraham exits, running for Simon.

Blackout.

Scene 7

MARY. "My ears have not yet drunk a hundred—" My ears have not yet drunk? Really? "My ears have not yet drunk."

"My ears have not yet drunk a hundred words
Of that tongue's uttering, yet I know the sound."

John knocks.

Just a minute! Come in!

John enters.

"My ears have not yet drunk a hundred words
Of that tongue's uttering, yet I know the sound.
Art thou not Romeo, and a Montague?"

JOHN. Good afternoon, Madame First Lady.

MARY. You came back!

JOHN. Well, I need the work.

MARY. Oh. I see. I've been practicing.

JOHN. I'm happy to hear.

MARY. And I made you something.

Mary hands John a large poster board. The audience cannot yet see what it says.

JOHN. What is this?

MARY. Oh just a silly little picture. It's not great, but I didn't have much time.

JOHN. You made this? For me?

MARY. Mhmm. Read it.

JOHN. John Wilkes Booth? In…raow—row—my—Romeo! John Wilkes Booth in *Romeo and Juliet*!

MARY. Sorry, my spelling is bad.

John reveals the poster. A quasi-badly mocked-up poster for a play that reads "Jonwilks Bootf in Row My Owen Gooly Yet."

JOHN. It's beautiful. You painted this?

MARY. Yes. I know it looks like my children did it, but I promise you I never go near my children.

JOHN. A poster of me. In the starring role. This is probably the nicest thing anyone's ever done for me.

MARY. Well, I just want you to know, Mister Booth, I'm sorry.

JOHN. No, Madame First Lady, I'm sorry.

MARY. No, I antagonized you.

JOHN. No, I antagonized you.

MARY. Well that's true.

JOHN. I know. I didn't mean to. I just meant to push you a little. Push you because I see what greatness you're capable of and I want you to get there.

MARY. Oh Mister Booth, I want me to get there too.

JOHN. Call me John.

MARY. Call me Mary.

JOHN. Mary.

MARY. John. Shall we continue where we left off last time? *The Tempest*? I think I finally understand subtext.

JOHN. Do you?

MARY. Yes it's like being inbred.

JOHN. How so?

MARY. Well, a character might say, "Chicken tummy time," when what they really mean is, "I'm hungry," only it doesn't come out quite right because they're inbred. Is that subtext?

JOHN. Well, not quite. Everyone uses subtext. Not just inbred people. Watch this: "I'm happy!" See how I said "I'm happy," but I said it very angrily?

MARY. Yes! Because your parents are siblings!

JOHN. No. Let's read the scene. You'll see what I mean. Ready?

MARY. Yes.

JOHN. "And for your sake
     Am I this patient log-man."

MARY. "Do you love me?"

JOHN. Stop. Let's try that again. Say it as if you mean it.

MARY. How?

JOHN. Look at me when you say it. Up here. Make eye contact with me.

MARY. Which eye?

JOHN. Both.

MARY. Okay. Wait, I'm getting dizzy.

JOHN. Read the line.

MARY. *(Reading.)* "Do you love me?"

JOHN. Now say it again. To me.

MARY. Do you love me?

JOHN. No. It's a question.

MARY. Do you love me?

JOHN. No. Don't think. Want. You're asking "Do you love me" because you want an answer. Want the answer, Mary.

MARY. Do you love me?

JOHN. More. Want it more.

MARY. Do you love me?

JOHN. Good! Now want it and fear it and know you're going to get it!

MARY. Do you love me?

JOHN. "O heaven, O earth, bear witness to this sound
    And crown what I profess with kind event
    If I speak true! If hollowly, invert
    What best is boded me to mischief! I
    Beyond all limit of what else i' th' world
    Do love, prize, honor you."

    John and Mary gaze longingly into each other's eyes.

MARY. How did you do that?

JOHN. What?

MARY. You made me believe what you were saying. You made it sound like you believed what you were saying.

JOHN. That's acting, Mary.

MARY. Get outta here.

JOHN. It's true.

MARY. But I'm so wet—er confused. How did you do that?

    John looks right at Mary.

JOHN. Well, I just picture someone I'm intrigued by. Someone I could feel myself being mad about. Someone who makes my heart flutter just by looking at them, talking to them, being near them.

    John takes steps towards Mary.

MARY. Someone I know?

JOHN. Yes.

MARY. Is it Louise?

JOHN. Who's Louise?

MARY. You don't know Louise? Everyone knows Louise! Nobody likes her, but everyone knows her. She puts ice cream on her—it doesn't matter.

JOHN. It isn't Louise.

John gets closer to Mary.

MARY. Oh. "I am a fool to weep what I am glad of."

JOHN. "Wherefore weep you?"

John is very close to Mary, about to kiss her. Mary is deeply lost in his eyes.

MARY. Line.

John kisses Mary's hand.

I don't think that's the line.

JOHN. No. It's the subtext.

MARY. Oh. I love acting. It's crazy. I'm all mixed up and confused. Maybe I'm inbred.

JOHN. The scene is over now. This is me, Mary.

John tries to kiss Mary. She pushes him away.

MARY. Mister Booth! Please! I cannot—

JOHN. Mary!

MARY. No. Mister Booth, please. If you care for me at all you will not do that.

JOHN. I'm only sorry I waited this long. Mary, you are…perfect. You are…

MARY. Please.

JOHN. I know! I sound stupid! That's the problem with being an actor, finding the right words in real life. I'll just say it plain. I'm in love with you. I love you, Mary. I love you.

MARY. Don't say that!

JOHN. Why not?! It's the truth! And you! You feel it too! I know you do!

MARY. Please! Leave me alone!

JOHN. Not until you tell me you love me!

MARY. I can't!

JOHN. Then tell me you don't!

MARY. I can't!

JOHN. Why? What's holding you back—your husband?

MARY. It's not my husband.

JOHN. Then tell me, please, I love you, and will understand.

MARY. Have you ever had a great day?

JOHN. Well, sure.

MARY. I mean a truly great day. The kind of day so great it imbues every single sad or boring or terrible day that came before it with deep meaning because from where you stand on this great day, all those days were secretly leading to this one. And you stand there, high on the hilltop of this great day, watching the sun set on your past, and it all looks so beautiful and so perfect and you think, "If only I could stay here, where I can see everything so clearly, where all of my hopes feel rewarded and all of my pain finally makes sense." But you can't stay there and the sad days and the boring and the terrible days aren't secretly leading anywhere.

JOHN. But they are. They're leading to more great days.

MARY. John, I can't afford any more great days. When great days are over, I break. It's why I left the stage. It's why I drink. It's why I married Abraham. He rescued me from that cycle of highs and lows by promising me a lifetime of steady, just fine days.

JOHN. Mary, don't close your heart to me out of fear. I can give you just fine, okay days too.

MARY. No you can't. You're full of great days. You are a great day. You're the best day I've ever had. Life with you wouldn't be a hill, it would be a mountain. It's too dangerous. I'll have to come down and I'll go mad, I'll fall apart, I'll die.

JOHN. Do you believe in past lives?

MARY. Huh?

JOHN. Past lives. I never believed in them until I met you. They say our souls live the same life over and over again until we get it right. Mary, I believe I loved you before. And I believe I let you go. And I believe if I let you go again we will live this same story again in our next life. And over and over again until we finally break this pointless cycle of torture and accept that we belong together.

MARY. Or maybe we've always ended up together and it's ended terribly and we'll continue this tragic story over and over again until one of us is wise enough and strong enough to end it.

JOHN. If that were true, you'd feel it!

MARY. Would I?

> *In the heat of the moment, John climbs onto the desk. Mary follows.*

JOHN. Yes! You'd feel it in your heart! If you don't feel it—if you don't love me, say it and I will leave and never come back! What's in your heart, Mary?! Tell me! What's in your heart?!

MARY. Blood!

JOHN. What else?!

MARY. Veins!

JOHN. What else?!

MARY. A pulmonary valve! And…

JOHN. And what, Mary?! And what?!

MARY. And love!

> *Mary and John kiss and embrace.*

I love you. I love you.

JOHN. I love you.

MARY. Oh, John. Take me away from here. Let's go now! I'm serious! Right now! Let's go!

JOHN. Where?

MARY. Canada!

JOHN. Canada?

MARY. I know it sounds crazy, but I've asked around, it's a real country just north of America, whatever that is. Let's go, now.

> *John and Mary get off of the desk.*

JOHN. Damn.

MARY. What?

JOHN. I wanted it to be a surprise. I got you an audition.

MARY. Audition? For what?

JOHN. The role of Georgiana in *Our American Cousin.*

MARY. But that show begins performances tomorrow. My husband has tickets.

JOHN. One of the actresses dropped out at the last minute to take care of her dead husband. They're having replacement auditions right now.

MARY. Oh John!

JOHN. Wait a minute! If you get the role, you'd take the play to the Canadian provinces and I could meet you there. Then when the play comes back to the States, you simply don't get on the train. You and I will stay in Canada and start a new life there!

MARY. Yes. Yes! Oh but my husband! He'll never let me audition!

JOHN. Does he need to know?

MARY. I guess not. He's always so busy with his special friend Simon, he won't even notice I'm gone.

JOHN. Who?

MARY. Simon. It doesn't matter. What shall I recite for my audition? Something from the Bible? Cleopatra?

JOHN. Relax, it's a character part.

MARY. Excuse me?

JOHN. So whatever you do will be brilliant.

MARY. I'll do the Nurse!

JOHN. Perfect!

MARY. I'll have to read from the book, I don't know it by heart! Help me find that book will you!

> *Mary and John look for the book. John opens a desk drawer and pulls out a gun.*

JOHN. Huh.

> *He examines it briefly and then sets it back in the drawer.*

We shouldn't arrive together. I'll go to the theatre now and let them know you're coming. I love you.

MARY. I love you.

> *John and Mary kiss. Unbeknownst to them, Louise appears*

in the window behind them and gasps at the shocking scene. John exits.

Did you hear that, Mother? I'm in love and I'm moving to Canada.

Abraham enters.

ABRAHAM. There are no more bottles in here Mary.

MARY. I was just looking for my book and then I'm going out for a walk.

ABRAHAM. You sure seem in a hurry for someone who's just going out for a walk.

Mary tries to leave, but Abraham blocks her.

MARY. Fine! I am going to Ford's Theatre to audition for a character part in *Our American Cousin.*

ABRAHAM. That starts tomorrow.

MARY. An actress dropped out at the last minute and John—Mister Booth got me an appointment to replace her.

ABRAHAM. I forbid you to go.

MARY. You promised if I took the lessons and a part came along—

ABRAHAM. I said we'd cross that bridge when we come to it!

MARY. Well we're at that bridge and I'm crossing it!

Mary tries to leave again; Abraham blocks her again. Mary punches him in the gut and he doubles over in pain. As Mary exits, Louise enters.

Hello Louise. We're all out of ice cream but if you're in the mood for something cold, help yourself to my husband.

Mary exits.

LOUISE. Mister President, are you all right?

Abraham nods.

I have something of grave importance to tell you. About your wife and…Mister Booth.

Blackout.

Curtain closes.

Scene 8

In front of the show curtain, Mary makes her way to center.

MARY. Hello! Hello, I'm here for my audition! I'm sorry I'm late, I got held up at home by my hus…by my…by a gay guy. Anyway, I'm here now and that's all that matters, right? Shall I take off my bonnet? My acting coach, Mister Booth, mentioned this is a character part. Georgiana. Is she a bonnet kinda gal? Well, I guess you see what I look like with a bonnet, you probably want to make sure "God, I hope she looks okay without a bonnet!" And that's your right. You have every right to that. So here, I'll take it off. Ta-da! Presenting Mary Todd—that's my name by the way, Mary Todd. Of course my married name is Lincoln but I'm not trying to use that to curry any favor. Mmm, curry, now I'm hungry! No. Uhhh, where should I start? Uh, yes! I will be reciting for you the role of Nurse from *Romeo and Juliet*. By William Shakespeare. And I'm realizing I forgot my book. I don't have the book. Oh, Mary. But I will improvise! Okay? Yeah, I'll just improvise here. But uh, okay, so—this is Nurse from *Romeo and Juliet*.

She speaks in what she thinks is a cockney accent.

Oi! Me name's the Nurse! And I seen that Romeo kissin' Lady Miss Juliet, I have. Wif me own two eyes! 'Course, I done a right good lot of kissin' in my time, I has! Loads of men, fresh offa them sailboats down at the dock. I close me eyes and I can still picture them men, comin' down offa them ships, them big balls pokin' outta the holes in their ripped-up trousers. I right like the smell of balls I do. But I don't kiss and tell. Not like Lady Miss Juliet, who's been kissin' and tellin' and kissin' some more! She killed herself today. Now I s'pose it's up to ol' Nurse to clean up the mess. Ah well, I still got me mem'ries. Good night.

She reverts back to her normal voice.

The end.

She bows.

Would you like something else? I'm better with a script, I promise.

Well, thank you for your time and I look forward to hearing from you! Oh, also! Should the part require it, you'll recall from my husband's inauguration I can put my legs behind my head.

Blackout.

Scene 9

Curtain opens to reveal Miller's Saloon. There's a bar with some stools, a café table with a couple chairs, and a piano. At the piano is Phil (a mannequin), behind the bar is Bill (same actor as Louise). At the bar is a drunkard, Kyle (same actor as Simon). Mary enters.

MARY. Hiya boys!

BILL and KYLE. Mary!

BILL. Where the hell ya been, Mary?

KYLE. Yeah, how come we never sees ya no more?

MARY. Fellas you'll never believe this but I'm in love!

BILL and KYLE. Whoa!

BILL. What's his name? Jack Daniels?

MARY. Nah! I don't need Jack, I've got John, John Wilkes Booth.

BILL. The actor?

MARY. Yes, Bill. The actor and the love of my life.

BILL. This calls for some celebratin'! How 'bout a number?! How 'bout one of your madcap medleys!

KYLE. Yeah!

MARY. I can't.

BILL. Come on!

MARY. I can't.

BILL. Please, Mary!

MARY. I fucking said I fucking can't! I have to save my energy. I'm making my acting debut tomorrow night in *Our American Cousin* over at Ford's Theatre!

KYLE. Wow!

MARY. Yeah, Kyle, it's wow! You're both invited, by the way. This just goes to show ya boys: Sometimes three continuous decades of quiet but unrelenting emotional pain can lead to something… pretty cool.

BILL. Does your husband know about all this yet?

MARY. Nope.

BILL. Well he's about to find out. Look! Here he comes!

> *Mary gets behind the bar. Abraham enters.*

Afternoon, Mister President.

ABRAHAM. Afternoon.

BILL. Your wife's not here. Haven't seen her since eighteen forty s—

ABRAHAM. No. I'm here for myself. Whiskey, please.

> *Bill hands Abraham a bottle and a glass. Abraham sits down at the café table. He pours himself a glass. John Wilkes Booth enters, spots Abraham, and goes to his table.*

Sit down.

> *John sits down.*

JOHN. Can I at least—

ABRAHAM. Be quiet, will you! I paid you to keep her busy so she didn't drink.

JOHN. That's what I've done.

ABRAHAM. I said I wanted her off the stage and out of my hair.

JOHN. That's what I've done.

ABRAHAM. An audition for *Our American Cousin*? How is that "off the stage"?

JOHN. It wasn't a real audition. I paid a child to sit in the balcony and pretend to be the director.

ABRAHAM. Why?

JOHN. I had to think of something! She wanted to skip town with me! Today!

ABRAHAM. And whose fault is that, lover boy?

JOHN. Well I'm sorry! Have you ever had to sit through her performances?

ABRAHAM. Yes.

JOHN. Then you know! I'm only human. And I am so sick of hearing about her madcap medleys and her years as a cabaret star.

ABRAHAM. I'm sorry? Years? As a star? She was never a star. She sang for six nights in an animal variety show that she paid to be a part of. Audiences hated her.

JOHN. I can see why! I can't stand reading lines with her, so we stop and I flirt with her, then I can't stand her flirting so I get her to read lines again and it just goes back and forth and back and forth until I reach a point where I'll do anything to shut her up, even if it means kissing that god-awful, disgusting mouth.

ABRAHAM. I'm so sorry.

JOHN. I retch all the way home.

ABRAHAM. It's gotten out of hand. People have seen you.

JOHN. Who?

ABRAHAM. Louise.

JOHN. Who the fuck is Louise?!

ABRAHAM. She saw you and Mary in each other's arms.

JOHN. Well good! Better they suspect me and Mary than me and you.

John grabs Abraham's hand. Abraham self-consciously pulls it away, gesturing to Bill.

ABRAHAM. John, please.

JOHN. Come on, it's been so long.

ABRAHAM. I know.

JOHN. It's not fair. The whole reason I'm doing this gig with Mary is to be close to you. I don't care about the money. I miss you so bad. Feel how bad Mommy misses her big, big boy.

John tries to pull Abraham's hand down under the table, but Abraham pulls away.

ABRAHAM. It's gotten out of control. Let's call it off, okay?

JOHN. Okay! I don't care about your stupid wife's drinking

problem. She's pathetic. Honestly, you should let her drink or have her put away.

ABRAHAM. Oh I am. I'm shipping her off in two weeks. To Bellevue.

JOHN. Bellevue?

ABRAHAM. It's a mental institution. I chose it because…

JOHN. Because what?

ABRAHAM. Because the patients there have the shortest life expectancy.

JOHN. Holy shit. Did you actually look into that?

ABRAHAM. Of course.

JOHN. God, you are so fucking hot.

John reaches for Abraham's hand, but Abraham pulls away.

ABRAHAM. John, please. I said let's call it off.

JOHN. You mean call it off with your wife, right? Not call it off with us…

Abraham doesn't answer.

You're not calling us off.

ABRAHAM. I am.

JOHN. No, you're not!

ABRAHAM. John.

JOHN. Where is this coming from?!

ABRAHAM. Shhh.

JOHN. Is it Simon?

ABRAHAM. What?

JOHN. Mary told me about Simon. Do you love him?

ABRAHAM. No!

JOHN. But you're fucking him.

ABRAHAM. Shut up!

JOHN. Oh my God. You are. You're fucking him.

ABRAHAM. I'm gonna go.

JOHN. Wait! I don't care that you're fucking him! As long as it's me you love, I don't care!

ABRAHAM. Look, John. You are such a great, great guy.

JOHN. No! Fuck you. Really? You are a fucking liar. I'm gonna tell everyone you're a fucking faggot.

ABRAHAM. Be quiet! What is wrong with you?!

JOHN. Nothing is wrong with me. This is what love is, Abraham. Love is hard work and consequences for your actions.

ABRAHAM. You need help, John! You are sick. We are not in love. We had sex like four times. And now I'm done with that.

Abraham starts to leave; John grabs him by the arm, tight.

JOHN. End this and I will end you.

Abraham breaks away from John's grip.

ABRAHAM. End yourself John. I'm the goddamn president of the United States. Who the hell are you? A pretty face and a fat ass. That's it. But your face is cracking and your ass is starting to sag. And what's left when those things are gone? Your talent? Your brothers got the talent. You got nothing. You are nothing. And you know that. You know you're on your way out so you're clinging to me for dear life. Well cling to someone else, John. I'm leaving.

JOHN. I'll let you do that thing again. That thing I said I didn't like. I'll do it. You can shove all three of them in me at once and I won't even scream this time.

Abraham tries to pay for the whiskey, then realizes he doesn't have money.

ABRAHAM. Goodbye, John! Shit! I don't—Do you have cash?

JOHN. Don't do this! You mean everything to me. Why would you throw this all away?

ABRAHAM. *(To Bill.)* I don't—I don't have cash, I can come back—

BILL. On the house.

ABRAHAM. Thanks.

JOHN. No! You will not leave me, Abraham Lincoln! You think Mary's going to ruin you? Just wait until I'm done!

ABRAHAM. You are just as pathetic as Mary.

JOHN. Fuck you!

> *Abraham exits.*

Wait! I'm sorry! No! Abe! Please!

> *John exits. Mary gets out from behind the bar.*

MARY. I'll be honest. That wasn't great.

> *Blackout.*

Scene 10

> *The curtain closes. We hear thunder and rain as Mary walks across the stage. Suddenly she runs into John.*

JOHN. Abe! Abraham! Mary? My darling, I have been searching for you everywhere! What are you doing out here?

MARY. I'm just out for a walk.

JOHN. Have you been drinking?

MARY. Yeah!

JOHN. Well thank God I ran into you Mary, I must see your husband. I…want to tell him about us.

MARY. Oh.

JOHN. The sooner I speak to him, the sooner we can leave and begin our new life together. But I need to know where he is.

MARY. But the play. What if I get the part?

JOHN. Oh. I—you didn't get the part, Mary.

MARY. Ohhh.

JOHN. I know. They said you were amazing! But they went with someone older. But Mary, listen! Listen to this: They want to build a whole new show around you!

MARY. No way.

JOHN. Yes! Isn't that wonderful news?! That's why I need to speak with your husband right now. Where is he?

MARY. I'll tell him.

JOHN. No!

MARY. Why?

JOHN. It's only right that I do it. Man to man. I just tried to see him at your house and he isn't in. You said something about someone named Simon?

MARY. Yes.

JOHN. Maybe he's there, at Simon's house?

MARY. Maybe.

JOHN. Where does Simon live?

MARY. I don't know.

JOHN. Think, Mary!

MARY. I really don't know.

JOHN. Damn! You said you and Abraham have tickets to *Our American Cousin* tomorrow, right?

MARY. Yes.

JOHN. Perfect. He'll have to see me there. I must go now and get everything ready for us. Not a word to your husband about any of this.

MARY. All right.

JOHN. I'll see you and Abe tomorrow night at Ford's Theatre.

MARY. Forb's Theatre!

> *John exits.*
>
> *Blackout.*

Scene 11

> *The curtain opens. A balcony facade is placed stage right. This is the booth at Ford's Theatre. Mary and Abraham enter and take their seats behind it.*

OFFSTAGE VOICE. Ladies and gentlemen, the president and first lady of the United States!

> *Abraham and Mary rise, wave, and smile. We hear applause.*

Mary and Abraham sit in silence, flipping through their programs. Mary looks around for John.

ABRAHAM. What are you looking for?

MARY. Nothing.

The lights dim.

We hear the play. Mary keeps looking around. Abraham signals her to sit still. Slowly, John appears from the curtain behind Mary and Abraham. John places his hand on Abraham's shoulder. Abraham jolts, startled.

JOHN. Shhhh.

ABRAHAM. *(Whispered.)* What the hell!

Mary jumps up from her seat; John sits in it, clinging to Abraham.

JOHN. *(Whispered.)* I love you! Please! Listen to me! I love you!

Mary, standing behind Abraham, procures a gun and shoots him in the back of the head. Mary drops the gun in John's lap. John and Mary stare at each other.

The lights come up, audience mumbling is heard.

MARY. Help! That man shot my husband!

John, in a panic, jumps off the balcony, off of the actual stage, and exits through the house. Louise rushes in to tend to Abraham and carry him offstage. Mary stands alone in front of the curtain, which closes.

I read in *Webster's Dictionary* the other day that mountains are formed by plates under the earth's surface that push up against each other until they buckle upwards and form a peak. Do you understand what that means? It means a mountain is just a valley under enormous pressure with nowhere to go but up. Now who does that remind you of? I was never on a mountain, I am a mountain!

Mary pulls off her dress to reveal a jazzy cabaret look.

Scene 12

Curtains open to reveal Mary's cabaret act. Simon accompanies her on piano.

SIMON. Ladies and gentleman, please welcome my friend, my collaborator, the love of my life, Miss Mary Todd!

Mary performs a madcap medley of songs spanning several genres and time periods. It is seven to nine minutes in length. The songs are meaningful to Mary and reflect her arc in some way. The medley ends. Blackout.

For information on licensing the medley arranged for the original Off-Broadway and Broadway productions, please contact Concord Theatricals.

End of Play

MUSIC AND THIRD-PARTY MATERIALS USE NOTE

Licensees are solely responsible for obtaining formal written permission from copyright owners to use copyrighted music and/or other copyrighted third-party materials (e.g. artworks, logos) in the performance of this play and are strongly cautioned to do so. If no such permission is obtained by the licensee, then the licensee must use only original music and materials that the licensee owns and controls. Licensees are solely responsible and liable for clearances of all third-party copyrighted materials, including without limitation music, and shall indemnify the copyright owners of the play(s) and their licensing agent, Dramatists Play Service, an imprint of Concord Theatricals Corp., against any costs, expenses, losses and liabilities arising from the use of such copyrighted third-party materials by licensees. For music, please contact the appropriate music licensing authority in your territory for the rights to any incidental music.

IMPORTANT BILLING AND CREDIT REQUIREMENTS

If you have obtained performance rights to this title, please refer to your licensing agreement for important billing and credit requirements.